The Bug Bus

by Carmel Reilly

illustrated by Pauline Reeves

OXFORD
UNIVERSITY PRESS

Bill ran to the big bus.

2

Bill got on as it set off.

The bus hit a lot of mud.

The bus did not go.

Bill got off the bus.

Bill hit a lot of mud.

It is no fun.

Bill got back on the bus.